# Violets Violins Violence

Sarah Wentworth

for Roxanne, my only constant, my only love

flight disrupted and destination becoming unclear
shrouded and dissolved into disbelief
   southward falling
inviting reason to clarify an absent destiny
empty handed and quieted by an instinct
   to ignore
boredom's disease devours desire
distracting any attempt at Zen
   dualities gray
    relentless

in case of emergency
   shoot to kill
the only way to survive
   myself
to be my own betrayer
accounting for displaced
   animosity
my inventory runs low
tracing back to myself
carving lines to replace
   what is lost

i can bury myself inside
    and survive
i memorize inflictions
    a loaded gun
poised for fire
  cornered
  wounded
fight or flight
fight or flight
    spite
seething till you cower
blanks are painful too

passion imprisoned by impropriety
arranged in moments courted
      by tension
allowing only so much to escape
      into flirtation
insinuation the only means to convey
      such treachery
chewing my thoughts, too sour to swallow

      single file
  an attempt to recreate order
defiled by lack of intention
   (attention)
collapsing back into the vacuum
   of a broken star
staring at the black waning moon
   sky
attaching poetry and nature
   to a cycle, a style
and grounding them
   inevitably in cliché

something about the way
it slides against my teeth
  repels me
to the dark it falls away
and i disregard its loneliness
no remorse inclines me to forget
  or forgive
given only what i can pry free

expulsion from dream state erupts
in a shower of doubt and anxiety
i want to sleep again
    in existence
this luxury is not mine
i am wide awake and stuttering
in the face of the day
i manage a sentence
whispered and throaty
for a first utterance
halting images cascade through
    the haze
i am silenced
there is cold in my breath
swirling in a subconscious well
deeper than i can see
   (am i drowning?)
i fight for a photograph of a past
i cannot remember or regret
   empty handed
struggling to emerge
held back by a nagging sense
   of nothingness
a souvenir of my earthly experience

i'm biting my nails
holding out for a last chance at freedom
(freedom only a label for chemical
concoctions at the wheel)
only lonely for lack of a better option
angry (hungry) for an antagonistic gouge
at my honesty
a challenge of my clarity
a laugh at my ferocity
i beg too softly
and can barely hear myself

  i separate inside a wonder
    and a whim
 who will win?
   i am running out
of running space
  distracted by a stripe
a white lie of formality

it's the middle that scares me
  (surrounded, mediocre)
unable to appeal to instinct
  preoccupied by ego
my last stand spent kneeling
aggressively destroying the evidence

a prisoner of myself
confined to this mortality
condemned to a knowledge
of the persistence of time
rummaging through the decayed
in hopes of retribution
denying a desperate yearning
to console myself in pain
mincing words to keep revealed
this hunger for extremes
restraint is hard to master (to muster)
screaming in spite of myself
i push through the wall
into a new beginning

centered in this moment
  a shiver relates my intimidation
there is a whisper attempt at calm
  before i run
unfocused on destination
  only aiming away
your kisses haunt my memories
a startling reminder of my humanity

with that glance
my imagination does cartwheels
dizzy and collapsing in the frenzy
a blank draws itself on me
   empty eyed
but disguised with a smile
  lying prone
  sprawled
a comfortable way to be ignored
recalling past occurrence
and equating it with complacence
   i arrive
   untied
and ready to play

   pursed lips
my warning not to proceed
stepping back to allow
  a breath
escaping into a sour disposition
to heal these tiny wounds
  stalling in the grass
to feel life between my toes
sudden urges replace worry

<u>disreputable</u>
a sneer that lasts a mile to nowhere
　wears a hole
attempting to unnerve
and arriving at dissolution
　a cringe
hesitation brings down the veil
and conforms a circle
with a missed gesture

<u>somnambulant</u>
simply stating the facts
promotes dissertations on ultimates
assumptions on their states
and an unraveling of progression
facing facts comes not
without objection
passing off aggression
   discretely
  with a smile
accumulating vices to adjourn
guilty into the night

still lost inside a web of miscommunication
do i dare decipher the message?
daunted by a power more fierce than fire
agony
driven into illusion to calm
and coerce sincerity
expanding time to decrease the tension
commotion waving wildly
for attention
masking order
with solitude
a second glance
empty space

a moment in distress
 another in distraction
interacting with words
 opposing thoughts
destroying the silence
 of imagination
and the dam purges
 in reaction to flooding
the cause and effect
 duality ringing in
for clarity
and the silence is
    resolved
   (reclaimed)

photography insinuates interest
are you interesting?
dissolve into the threshold
if incidents
reminded all the time
of imperfections resolved
by attractions at the basest level
sweating independence
dropping hints
indiscreetly
without shame

in anger and in hunger
in the basest and ugliest
    portrayals
    there is still
the fascinating beauty
    of existence
the glaring truth of life
and the disillusioning grandeur
    of our limitations

<u>new day revolution</u>
reevaluating my purpose
 (a frantic grasping)
amateur indecision
 no amount of practice
makes it easier
 or more attainable
insufficiently narrating
 these moments of self deception
and self deprecation
 almost angrily
almost aware of the irony
 almost intent on settling
but never willing to give in
 even in the darkest hour
 before dawn
when the sky seems beaten
and the sun has lost for its last time
   i await the rising
anticipating the revolution of a new day

i get quiet sometimes
and listen to the wind
whispering
in innocence of this sadness
the trees answer my sighs
and wave to the wind as
it tells my story
to the clouds
the rain and my tears mingle
and play on my cheeks
racing to the ground
and the wind follows me home

we talked the talk
and you lived the lie
but just like me you were
    born to die
you said you would
then we said goodbye
but just like me you were
    born to die

i try never to say never
    but i did it again
if i ever let go of this rope
i look forward to the sorrow
     of the fall
falling faster than the
horizon-eaten sun

i discovered my happiest day
and now it can happen again
a revolving door dream
keeping this silent picture
on my screen

an oafish grin
teeth wrangling for position
　but sincere
an uninhibited display
　achingly honest
and therefore beautiful

i shook hands with that man
   as he clenched his teeth
and darted his eyes through
         the crowd
   the lack of interest oozed
divulging the lie of his words

slipping across your midnight
you claim you've got a world
    of time
you count the minutes
but never your blessings
  at this rate
you'll never fly
 you only have to die once
but you can't tell your own
  tale
i can't seem to break your code
 so i'll take a stab of your heart
your nightfall conceals all
  but you know we're apart

i try to preserve the snowflake
      on my tongue
    but i can't help it
      i melt it
that's the nature of my heat

a quiet but inspired creation
as ink falls into line
i love the scratch of the pen
engraving the paper
and the way i slur my words

there's a flame
on the moon tonight
it takes light
and devours the sun
it wanders in and out
of the clouds
it remembers when
it didn't have to
thanks for leaving
the moon tonight
i'll never doubt you again

a silent stuttering vivid glow
i glisten in the window
on my way home
disappearing acts of nature
and the scenery becomes stark
long and vast and infinite
but describable, familiar
and almost comfortable

i'm swinging from a tree
in the trembling of the
    moonlight
where twilight feigns
    daylight
and the stars whisper
   like librarians
    as they leave

i go through the walls
as a ghost in my dreams
i continue to fascinate myself
with the mirror of sleep
in front of my face
and the ragged breath of daylight
on my pillow

people who hesitate
also have a tendency to rush
as a measure of extremes
in coital dance:
the air on my neck
and the whisper cloud
across the moon

i felt it again
with a sorrowing pang
if i hadn't ignored myself
i'd have you gone by now

the door opened
i stepped out
Midland seized me
with its dry smell
of oil and slow death
a breath away from loneliness
there was thunder miles off
and the electric glow
of lightning in the air
i almost fell in love

i try and yet am unaware
   the bell rings
and in a second the air
   changes color
and the spectrum of sound
   intensifies
the distraction welcome
until i become aware of it
   the second bell
     and light fails
leaving shadows where i stand
pencil shavings crunching at my feet
   i follow the beat of my heart

frequently reiterated "facts"
  marching in
forcing questions
antagonizing cautious minds
centering the unpleasant nature
of confinement and mediocrity
  directly in step
  left right left right
  my heart screams
  "break the pace"
  fall out of step
fall
a disgrace to my own morality

this ancient light entices me
    from sleep
i count the constellation
 diamonds in dreams

half forgotten moments carry me along
while i'm being let down
softly crossing this path
as on eggshells, barefoot, in the dark

this season's burden is on its way
out
delicately breathing towards
the west
there's a halo sun climbing down
the sky
a sharp inhale to remember

there was a misunderstanding
    a miscalculation
i find it hard to believe in the
pecan tree in the backyard
it is only tangible while i am
    awake
when i am alive
 in dreams i walk through it
in dreams i do not fear
 in dreams i am assured
and the value of existence
is exponentially more

i stopped at the window
pressing my face against
the cool glass
my breath makes opaque
the spot just before my eyes
the distortion almost surprises me

i dispense words
they roll gumball style
through the chemistry
　called brain
i chew on them
enjoying the flavor till
　it is gone
then i spit them out

an exercise in restraint
unasked questions are
seldom satisfied
still i hide
my dark eyes stare
empty back at me
and the mirror seldom lies

why is this enough to draw a tear?
aren't there other mountains waiting
aren't there other words to rhyme?
terrified but insulated
  there are others
   take your time
thirsty but satiated
there are other walls to climb

just keep playing
there's nothing for saying
i am washed clean out
by the tide

it keeps falling
that may be a product
of its heavy weight
there's no use in calling
  they are deaf
  to their fate
there's no use denying
there's dirt on this name

there are empty pages everywhere
  but i'd never dare
  to fill them all myself
  i watch and wonder
  we are the lost
  we are the found
isn't wonder an amazing sound

i dream i can breathe under water
and i fill my lungs with liquid
for air
sharp inhales of the dark water
i feel full and heavy
like awakening from a deep sleep
lids drooping, i sink
floating down
as a cloud to fog
and stare up to the light
until i catch dawn, red handed,
climbing through my window

powered by the subtext
  the night ignited
and a delicate pretense
  collapsed in the wake
all but matter
created and destroyed
  in a wink

wrapped in the emotion
of the sound
lost against the static
recognizing limitations
but refusing to let them in
searching to find a way to
silence this inner doubt
reflexively reviving guilt
a habit learned far too well
and i find i am searching again
how do i justify it this time?
(a window left open with
an eight story fall)

in this minute i remember
destiny's a former friend
my own whimsy drags me under
below the water line again
grasping silt between my toes
startled to remind myself
where mythos failed
you have prevailed
finding me an open door
to push myself through
to keep this water from pooling
to keep everything clear
allowing me to come up
once more for air

i can't remember how you forgave it
but i know where you got it
i know where it's from
lyrical dreaming
hysterical screaming
girls in white dresses
girls wearing glasses
all of them an image
of me

i will accelerate
accumulating speed
arousing my suspicions
of a perception of an early grave
i will accommodate these apprehensions
applying the brake
appealing to a sense of self preservation
suppressing the urge to
attempt to break sound

closer now and almost reaching
in her eyes i've lost the glow
she seeks me out and uses mirrors
to entice me into her again
this reflection leaves me empty
sullen, lost, and far from sleep
if i could keep this moment spinning
surely she would let me go
i would spiral out and redefine
the architecture of her grasp
loosening her fingers from me
finding comfort finally in me

i tremble as i unfold
these pages
remember these words
i dreamed there were
roses in cages
bleeding to white
to be free

<u>diving</u>
i was diving
and your letters lied
submerged in mind memory rows
i am talking, but i didn't know
are there words to enslave this thought?
can you justify this to me?
can i believe in the sunrise?
can i create these moments on my own?
i can sense the fear of doubt
i can sense the trap of doubt
i caress this fatal emotion
and pacify this interrogation
i will follow
the shadows from the grey
of noon
into the silver of day

<u>hiding</u>
there are two sides to this face
of mine
the jekyll and the hiding
cheeks pinked
by a rushing wind
i am ten again
with mud between
my toes
and a halo of sun
on my hair
i wink at the tadpoles
as they flit around
my ankles
i know what they
will become
not princes
i reach for his hand
and we go straddling fences
bumping elbows
trading smiles
sneaking glimpses
we tumble in the grass
in three years
it's just memories
and we pass on the street
and lie to ourselves
and sometimes he looks back

<u>atlas</u>
i stumble from the weighted
shoulder
sinking, falling, tumbling down
i am left reflecting, broken
to journey injured
on my own
if i can get this weight above me
hold it like a triumph
high
then i can walk this road
before me
masking fears
with a humbled frown

## A kiss
to tour it
to sail towards the
brightest star
against forceful wind
where despair
and ecstasy are
fair-weather friends
gradually giving way
to temptation
carefully applying
pressure to the wound
careful not to finalize
the last circulation
smooth surfaces
make comfortable beds
for your stone
for your alone
i christened your morning
with a kiss

<u>enemy</u>
i am an arch enemy
fanning the flames
of malcontent
raining on parades
drowning kittens
in their own water dishes
and yet you always open
your door when i knock
and welcome me
into your warm kitchen
where i promptly poison
you meat
and still you sit at your table
and devour the kill

<u>green</u>
i am hiding in a young world
where nothing ever passes
gratitude and differences aside
gathering violets
there's no one surprised
your fingers are green
the clouds gleam white

there are a hundred things
i never should have said
and i recall only fragments
of why
selective (corrective) memory
announcing what it will
instead of reflect
i will absorb

i can't define every word
but you know i'll try
that's what i do
we'll never know why
i'll ask you some questions
and answer myself
filling words with pages
to keep on a shelf

my lips are still wet
from that soft caress
i wipe them backhanded
and follow the dress

i've got a synergy
you've tried
to duplicate
you know better
we're bitter
there's no time
to wait

<u>unspoken</u>
you know i don't believe you
but you keep spinning
there's something i should
have said from the beginning
you'd have taken it for granted
it's the picture i wanted
not this

<u>translator</u>
she doesn't speak english
that's what i heard
that's what i was told
she won't understand us
her winters are cold
the prisms are illusions
of light
not tangible monuments
to what is right

this is an unauthorized
  thought process
don't argue with the past
hide your glasses from
  yourself
the red is deliberately
  darkening
the red is obediently
  darkening
absorbing light where it can
  radiating what it can
arbitrating what it can

<u>rot</u>
red meat spoils
sullying countertops
where (wear) blood leaks
watered down
to pool at my feet
swimming with parasites
i cannot decontaminate
this love
but it will exist
despite decay

i have wandered all my life
through the days and years
searching for something i held
  in my hand
something so soft i could barely
  accept it
in these words i have found it
-myself-
from a darkness of my own creation
i hid from what i was desperate
  to unveil
but i can see it now
  it is here
  i am here
these words are my mirror
and in this reflection i can see
where i thought they had dulled
there is still wonder in my eyes
where i thought it had grown cold
there is still love in my heart
and though i am still, from myself, apart
there is confidence that this journey there
  will be enough

<u>trip</u>
loss of concentration
crashing to the floor
 cracked
but not lost to the dust
only subjected to its
unpleasant penetration
 meditation
draws me back to my
sense of self
and i tend to my wounds

obligations self imposed
kicking me towards
the proverbial early grave
bitterness retreats to a corner
to simmer in disgust
and pry, crowbar style,
at my sense of self satisfaction

{crouching}
i shudder at your lack
of conviction
you flinch and run
loud noises ricochet
haunting you into a
corner
face buried in a cold
wall
back exposed for stabbing

<u>sunk</u>
underneath a wall of green
　it splays open for
your viewing pleasure
mask and make up
cracks in the smiles
　of disdain
who can scream
　for want of nothing
my only true love
　nothing
is funny all over again
that which is unknown
　can only chip
at the block of ice
　in the veins
tack it on the green wall
watch it melt away

<u>wrong</u>
she withered her way home
only shortly peeking over
her shoulder (a last glimpse
of perceived freedom)
she's grasping for serenity
and leaving the water's turmoil
(and leaving the warmth of
the waves) she never dares
  look forward
  only side to side
confusing left with wrong

<u>overcome</u>
kiss, eye open
 (tentative)
lashes brush against
moist warm flesh
 (a blush)
i am skin deep
i watch this overcome
 me
i am trapped in desire
unsatisfied
i whisper in the shadows
 i've tried
but it has overcome me

with cruelty and lies
i tether myself to my
 reflection
only laughing to destroy
 silence
only breathing
to contaminate what
has called me its own
struggling tightens the knots
 in my stomach
no amount of purity can save
 me from myself
accosting faith
 backhanded
swiftly tossing off
the garments of a lost age
 to run face first
 into the sun

filling in the blanks
  where i can
moments with no time
  expand through
  breaths
wrapping snow
around my ankles

cringing at the collapse
of my glass house of cards
left unguarded only minutes
destruction
an inevitability of creation

cold blast
and a withering word
a beat against a stain
systematically rotating
in a careless wander
a tributary path to oblivion

a trilogy of chords
pervasive in manner
marching to the beat
of the only drummer
whispering to my veins
empty

i am not sated
sighing mixes emotions
and stakes a claim
on my position in the stars
claiming to govern myself
(false before whispering)
i agree to the terms

can you sense that
i have had enough
that i am fading
i whisper to the trees
 to fall
but they do not exist
 for me
and my power is lost

searching for a voice
  (a vice?)
i careen carelessly
trampling daisies
  as i erase time
  (time erases me)
i have already forgotten
  my eyes

montpelier rolls off
 my tongue
i am already gone
 caving under a harsh
response
 i cradle my ego
couldn't soften the blow
 i creep back up the stairs
wary of every breath
 i am cold as snow

i condemned time
for wandering
i will not be still
expecting more
defiles what i have
i arrange thoughts
alphabetically so i can
think on something else
diversions befriend my
subconscious
crossword puzzles
excite me

almost enough
closer to the center
inscribe your moment
here
aching for solutions
in the sand
gritty in my nail
dig it out
deeper the torment
softer the lies
blood comforts
the lost calm

processing possibilities lends
a comforting distraction
in excess, i find redemption
undesirable
distractions make camp
in the dirt of desperate states
moments of weakness
implying a necessity to ignore
this is the space where awareness
rears its head
try to ignore that
processing possibilities
leads to a vacancy

<u>utopia</u>
the catalyst involves himself
with the nature of things
devising the most perfect plan
solving the riddles
in time
sunsets are inevitable
so it seems
but the ancient Greeks knew
that utopia was nowhere

only now is it clear
watery and diluted to appease
subjective happiness to replace
 a moment's disgrace
 boiling rapidly
in the pot that called
 the kettle black

snipe the wind
adjoin it to your
vast collection of
indiscretions
rhyme it with courage
its angular limbs
clumsily embracing
the moment
subtraction makes it less
tradition gives it class
stained with blood
hanging broken

<u>senses</u>
running from this glass skin
staggering to pronounce
 this song
ask me how i smell you here
 in my secret dark
use the slender tongue
 to find your meal
a page of my books
unfolds for you to devour
build me a rainbow
to climb over with you
 be my brother
be my avenue of sound
listen through the lace
of my words
and know me

tonight the skin beneath melts
into the nuisance of explanation
heavy pillows make soft the journey
but the roots integral to growth
are sparse and falling out of shape

aided and abetted by the
  noiseless black
  slink into place
my voice has been eaten
by your gluttonous ear
never defining infinity
for its impossibility
roaring into violence
for its cold comfort

prick and burst
the sun blisters brown
hazy photographs blush
 burning
cinders trap  and oxidize
volcanic flushing rivers to stream
tertiary floundering
breeze breaks out into swirls
 of dust
cascading whipped
 and whirled
breath falls flat
shatters, cracks
trickles to drains
spiraling towards a
reflection of what once
 was alive

<u>time</u>
the hourglass drips sand
piling into an illusion
of a concept yet untamable
untraceable by all accounts
so formally held as a constant
intentions are meaningless

out of awareness i thrive
existing visually for a physical
expression of the voyage
i have fallen from
warped and rattled free
from society's black shadow
i walk across the reddest sea
into the warmth of mother's smile
"you've gone astray"

<u>exhale</u>
i burn the leaf
that has drifted down
past function
frazzled and torn
the obituary soothes
frail understanding
of the occurrence
tantalized by the scent
the brethren for make circle
to quicken false pretense
the net is torn
this eternity will
encompass all

<u>starved</u>
viciously instinctual
ravenous for a morsel of truth
i'd kill them all if i saw
some answer in death
pacifism a product
of the knowledge
of defeat in suffering
reality a whisper of what
i want it to be
settling for what i can know
too little to satisfy
keep searching
for the vanity of it

earful of noise
a space between forever
and absence
squeamishly converting
mind to matter
each hour spends so quickly
each minute everlasting
concept of now marbled
with the acceptance of a past
employing only what is known
to map my path
the quicksand's hunger
engulfs me

sinking slowly
against my will
falling down
to kill this ever present
falseness of existence
the elation of hate
trapping sanity
in a pretty glass box

i feel the blood rush in
turning red from blue
hot, sticky and sour
complete with this
twinging in my womb
this unclaimed umbilical calling
cross stitched and labeled
  with selfishness
i can destroy what i can create
  i can destroy this
embryonic concoction
  within
craving complacence
only to find that sometimes
it is easier to create than to destroy

taken from the water
flopping to adapt to a distance
partnering with an individual
and  society's lack of progression
truth is a shot in the dark
coasting, trailing, skidding
  into fear
  fear of what
our condition contaminates
  any hope
crafting a clutter of conspicuous
  echoes
denial a soft pillow to catch
and soak up the tears

Stop!
gravity release me
into the certain death
vacuum of space
i won't mind the
lack of air
disease won't give in
i suffer though
i do not believe
in sin
insist in a refinery
to clean me
they are false
these words
fall farther from the
inclination to reveal
theorems
when reality,
too subjective,
can't be grasped

you slide inside
slipping through the barriers
 of flesh
 i cry
i want to indulge
and escape all at once
 so i let my body go
and drift into subconscious
wishing only to maintain
 a piece of myself
 a tiny morsel left behind
 as you devour the rest
 spitting as you chew

subtlety not my best suit
i rake in varieties of emotions
  scraping and bruising
   on the way
where do i hide from myself
depleting softly my deeper yearnings
caressed by the colder breeze
sailing by uninsured
but foolishly hopeful

confined to the solitude of self
my fantasies have boundaries
  thick as silences shared
wondering how emptiness tastes
  i decline interpretation
  it only leads to trouble
misreading the text is my secret
your expression priceless beneath
  those lashes
i have lived within long enough

<u>crunch</u>
glass beads shatter between my foot
   and rough dirt
disaster contains itself in your smile
   and compelled by red
i alleviate the weight of contrition
   against the floor my cheek
cools in the carpet of contempt

i claim this body as my own
i will no longer rent to
   the highest bidder
vacancy more appealing than use
too many intrusions have
left me trampled
i have become the
belly of the beast
   a decoy
diverting affections
i want to die alone

brutality grins through
   toothless gums
no sister could comfort this
   tear
entertained beneath falling angels
laughter echoing emptiness
   nature knows no good
   or evil
concerned only with the
regeneration of existence
  partial not to the
  human condition
only driven by itself

<u>photograph</u>
soft exposure with a simple kiss
leaving behind sentences
broken by lust
in between tumbling hair
and fumbling hands
can't resist the content
of this negative
instigating a print
to hold close the memory
of this moment

clumsiness scatters me across
the floor
blame cast out to save
from embarrassment
as i bleed from empty wounds
a warning form around the corner
darker than the nook behind my bed
peeking into vile pasts
i am running scared

my sense of smell is tangible
i can taste the sunset on your skin
slowly i drive myself further down
the empty road
wind pours through my veins
and i read the signs
each one screams STOP
i cannot obey
i must move further past me

<u>head on collision</u>
crouching away from your stare
my lungs discard gases with no purpose
excitement tries to pry inside
denied
allying with my heavy heart
i collide with your dream state
fully conscious of my certainty
scarred by nature's even hand
i anticipate this long mile
hoping for some rain

<u>bonfire of my vanity</u>
lighting myself on fire scatters through
ragged tired emotions
inspiring immaturity
screaming scratching
at the back of my throat
gasping inside darkened windows
mistakes filter forth
memory realizing its ultimate purpose
cancerous questions make themselves
available for examination
against my will
close my eyes for quiet
sleep for a thousand years

willowy she walks away from me
  my love
melting into blue as she fades away
  i am gray
  i miss her
moist against my cheek
fluttering
unconscious of her charm
her scars that match my own glisten
in eyes that watch for meaning

she crept in bloody
by her own hand
running instead
of falling flat
no more school bells
come back from that
moment
you'll see sooner
this way than that
i'll keep your flame

explanations are lost on today
no calm can come of flooded banks
whirlpool dragging down
i hear death reaching for you
i will resist, even as you draw it near

<u>neighbors</u>
those floor level with the top
of the stairs
stare empty
a relentless reminder
of the lack of progression
replacing thought
with aggression
curiosity cascades
through concrete teeth
falling floor level
into stagnant air

it is almost a premonition
and your pretty face
isn't beautiful at all
we piss in the wind
ever aware of the futility
let's talk small
and walk big

<u>voice</u>
there is an utterance
on its way out
i cannot place
  if it is a laugh
  or a scream
it rattles its way free
from my throat
it turns out to be a song
i was wrong all along

tossing off this flagrant grin
falsified for your protection
i search to eradicate (emulate)
these emotions
sulking in the dark
i find you empty
waiting to be filled
your only redemption
i harvest each fleck of skin
piecing together my own image
of this arrogance, this lack of imagination
if i instigate each touch
i will not be filled
i will resent each breath
falling from lips i cannot reach
is it too bitter to share?
the constant pulse of blood
through veins disappoints me
i cannot stop
individual regurgitation of pasts
does not interest or enlighten
when received in malcontent
destroy me and i will reconvene
in a space of my own

subtlety not my best suit
i rake in varieties of emotions
scraping and bruising
on the way
where do i hide from myself
depleting softly my deeper yearnings
caressed by the colder breeze
sailing by uninsured
but foolishly hopeful

soft exposure with a simple kiss
leaving behind sentences
broken by lust
in between tumbling hair
and fumbling hands
can't resist the content
of this negative
instigating a print
to hold close the memory
of this moment

when i told you
it was all or nothing
 you knew
what you had to do
you've never closed
 a door
so softly

<u>do it</u>
when you pointed
  your gun
  at my face
i was surprised
i had always thought
i would die alone
  i dared you
to squeeze a little
  harder
you can do it
pull that trigger
if you do it now
i promise to love you
for the rest of my life

i attended that funeral
i was the only one who
didn't cry
i was too busy screaming

**my prayer**
if i should die before we wake
maybe you will
finally take your ghost
 with you

<u>go away</u>
you came to me
when you saw me
with him
talking about how
he would never
be able to replace you
how he could never be you
i said "i know,
 and thank god"

if i wake up and you are
still fucking here
i will tear you apart
i said go
i did not mince words
i am not getting in your
car again

you are that
dream that
will never
come true
my lips
turn blue
as i slip
beneath
the waves
of desire
drowning
i don't think
i will
wake up

<u>umbrella</u>
stop your raining
this is my parade
this is my victory
march
i finally washed my
hands of you
but you are still
lingering beneath
my nails
maybe i should bite
them off

you are always
telling me what
    i mean
but you are
translating the wrong
    text
when i write
it is not always
about you

you whispered
"i love you"
and i wanted
to pull
the dagger
from my back
and plunge
it into your heart
you are a lie
and somehow
i let you lie next
to me
am i really that
desperate?

<u>puzzled</u>
and you thought your apologies
could glue me back together
when you had already
misplaced most
of the pieces
you are arrogant
and you are not mine
anymore
and i will me missing pieces
but i will not be missing you

<u>love</u>
is like riding
a horse
even as you
lie out of
breath
mangled
and bloody
in the dirt
you have to be
thinking
of how to climb
back up

i splashed in your puddles
you made me so wet
i had to take off my clothes
you stood facing the wall
while i unbuttoned
and peeled
i put on your shirt
it hung below my knees
when you faced me again
your eyes clung to my hips
and your lips came to my cheek
i brushed you away
as long as i could
"not again, please"
but you are plugged
your ears
and did it anyway

i wake up and wonder what i have done
it is always too easy to resist
when they say
"you're so pretty"
 i laugh
that's all they will ever see
but i fuck them anyway
  then run away
change my name
but you caught me sneaking
out the window this time
and begged me to stay
your cock and your ego
  needed stroking
  and i was bored

you put your hand in my hair
and forced me to face you
you want an explanation
  i want to run away
i saw you leave her room
you knew i would fight back
but you never thought i'd fight
  like this
i'm walking through this door
and leaving you the key
don't think i will not look back
don't think i will be back

you ask me to put
 out my cigarette
because it is killing me
 well so are you
can i put you out too?

the safety is off
point your gun
at me
my armor
is not bullet proof
i can only take one

<u>your eyes</u>
i roll my socks
down
there is a bruise
just below
my left knee
tender like your
touch
you lace your
fingers
through my hair
slipping down to
my neck
my socks are off
your eyes are on

i speckle the canvas
not committing to a solid notion
just yet
i want to climb this tree
that was born from my pen
before i cement its colors
before i confine the contents

fifteen minutes passed
 i refocused the lens
framing and lighting are key
the sun crept lower
and the moon made its presence
 known
click click click
the shutter speaks a language
i have only begun to translate

the time is set
pistols at dawn
load your weapon
carefully
that's live ammunition
there is no friendly caliber
when you take your aim
make sure you mean it
there's no going back
once that finger moves

<u>mixed drink</u>
i crack the cubes of ice
with a slap of the back
of a spoon
it stuttered for a note
but reported with a dull clink
the ice splits readily
unaccompanied
by spoon song
a capella
the snap is like brittle bone
i drop the palm of my hand
and encourage gravity
to its weary duty
ice falls to the glass
with a shiftless brand
of competence
bordering thought lines
mixing emotions

<u>straddling</u>
back and forth across
the great divide
we can't decide
which side we're on
i'll take the seaside
with you at the bedside
while we are outside
the sun shines for us

it is a left-handed conclusion
  that sideways works
in paper position
i write across my own words
  and they hide beneath
  my pen-clutching fist
  until i am done

i stand between the yellow lines
that is where my pen writes
i cover my ground in ink
footprints spell my route
i map lines with a stick of dynamite
my fingers tremble for fear of loss

as this wheel spins
i am hypnotized
by the line it creates
even backwards the progress
remains the same
 i have to jump
and tumble and bruise
if ever to walk again

<u>civil war</u>
i am dramatic enough
to be prematurely battle-worn
the naïve kind of tired of it all
the kind that moves forward
even against the tide of insecurity
and is strengthened by the powerful
weight of resistance

this collaboration is pregnant
with the pieces twins
oh metaphor, you entice me
i want to win
but first to begin
that is your stare that bends
me into thirds
to deserve your quench
to my thirst

role playing
i twisted my finger
around my wrist
i am part of this
this cast of
spotlight
the single x
i portray myself
and act the rest

i see my face in mirrors and pictures
and am not aware of myself
the image seems a vague
interpretation of what
this architect has built

<u>shutter speed</u>
i capture light in pixels
a language of geometry
 and sight
and wrap seconds
 in frames
 to replace
the need for words

it is this dark
that is the brightest
in negatives
a flare without
a shield
the backwards
color
makes food
for dreams

i don't need to back off
just pace my movement
with the left right march
of compulsion
there are times
 when the count is off
it is easy for a clock to lie

<u>cannibal</u>
hot, sticky, sweet
your breath poured
down my throat
you taste of honeysuckle
scorched by the sting
of the sun's tongue
rotting on the vine
i want to eat you alive

<u>greedy</u>
you were a habit
that could only break me
and you considered it
you solemn duty
you split me in two
and took the larger
half for yourself

i prefer the company
of this pen
and this paper
to you
they do not talk
back
or tell lies
unless i do

when i gave it to you
it was still beating
however faintly
you managed
to destroy that too

this has been
my slowest
death yet
you keep teasing
one more breath
from me
against my
living will

carrying a gun
is serious business
you've got to shoot
to kill
without conviction
you are only aiming
at yourself

this valentine
comes early
and without guilt
i enter the silence
heavy with words
and we sleep in the
skin we have divined

the color explodes
  from those eyes
the sharpness makes cuts
  in my heart
i embrace the edge
  despite the pain
of knowing
  i enter your dreams
as you leave

i started a fire
in the seclusion
of my headphones
provocative words
  with music
to make them whole
but whole before
i even knew it
there is poetry
i cannot ignore
in the notion
of the chords
poems aren't
always made
  of rhymes

<u>plagiarism</u>
i'm writing songs
that have already
been written
and still i am smitten
with these words
i have known all along
that this is fitting
and i'm getting ready
to carry it on
from play to play
from pay to day
i'll get away
with it

it's on the back
of the record cover
we're passing every test
even if by the skin
of our teeth
cheek to cheek
our waltz finally in step
this caper drapes our shoulders
in the cool dawn of september

## weather

the white night hangs thickly
arousing the fireflies
stinging my eyes
i have been tossed by sunset
into creation's most beautiful
creature
winter climbs a wall of clouds
clinging to architecture
for a better view
succumbing to a warm breath
she backs down the fire escape
towards the possibility
of extinguishing snow for steam

that sound runs me through
so i lie
no one knows what is real
where i hide
cascading facades grinding
idiots frolic
no sense to make them cry
i am what is wrong with me
i am that little nothing
whispered in your ear
not so sweet
where i grope for meaning
you grasp for the next
big distraction
we'll never reach
our destination
death will stop us flat

push it out
expel
pleasantly aborted
grease on the
tile diamond
stained wet
without regard, regret
unavailable to
experience it alone
bag it up
for safe keeping

slithered under your breath
swept through
anxiety calls for more
i sweat between these
moving walls
imposing conversations seep
into consciousness
flustered, frightened
where is my nightfall?
can I own myself again?

<u>dictionary</u>
fumbling through the index
a paper cut reminder
a sting
and my quest is left unfinished

furnishing thought with
a recapitulation
of a former lessen
does memory serve?
a question answered
a seconds elation

her smile is glass
as I walk along rows
of teeth
toward longing
each toe slicks across
spit
reminds me of piano
keys
down the slide of
her tongue
i find my way through
those words
deciphering on the
way down

we go on building this contagious wall
like sleeping children
oblivious to the nightmares
when we wake
dirty secrets
like dirty hands
smudge the clear windows of thought
with scandalous breath
trying in vain to keep
our dream house clean
each day i breathe the vapors
of the humid morning
dark before the sun
and quiet
light the fire
we will consume the world
with the flame of our being

i wish to tear this ticking clock
out of mind
i will tear away the gears
and springs
to dissect this time
this minute
are your eyes too closed
to dialate
to register
to admit this image is ours
over wanting
and disdain for flesh
after her my place is last
lost for who i couldn't stand to be
has this morning's sun burned
my retinas
to blind me against my art
i was wrong to speak
it only stagnates the air
and suffocates my letters
-enunciate-
my tongue, dry
longs to be free

soul sad sounds
caress the air,
flow into my heart
resisting the stars is futile
they live in my eyes
the beauty of the voice
the simplicity of the word
the honesty of the tears
hurts to stare into such purity
the blinding black sincerity
can sense fear

my alibi weakens
under the pressure
of constant denial
can i facilitate
a new comfort?
gouging out the
eyes that pry
admiration deepens
falling short still
a little gasp for air
only to try again
flick away the specks
of dirt
can't help but want
to keep it clean

entering the silence
intimidates my resolve
insecurity placates me
back doors slam into me
motionless
instances of growth evolve
from this emptiness
embracing silence
becomes the quest for
enlightenment
I want to skip through
emotionless

grasping the wing
tearing it free
losing compassion
to instinct
lighting fires where
i can
to smolder
only in denial
can i sleep

her ghost is still in the backseat
the attempt at subtlety loses itself
casting doubt
illuminating allusions
to yesterday's parade
the stilts make it seems taller
but the underbelly is still exposed

ignoring the frailty
of the situation
an unwanted side effect
of acts of contrition
somewhere there is salvation
from myself
left ungranted

over my shoulder
i can feel it
my savior
calling me down
calming me down
fast as i can fall
too far for capture
rushing into silence
fear lost
at last

it is rushing in
not bothering with
niceties
or veils
contorting your voice
staining the atmosphere
i wrap my hair tight
around my finger
and ignore that vagueness
you project
it rushes out more slowly
and tempers my mood

frightened by such a
sudden desire
immersion the only
 answer
failing to persuade
tied up and touching
 toes
hair pulled tight
 hard
 wet
 empty